Making

The **Shift** From

Self-Employed to

Business

Ownership

Joy L. McLaughlin-Harris

Founder of Touch of Joy Dream Academy

Making the Shift from Self-Employed to Business Ownership

Printed in the United States of America

Editor: Tamika L. Sims, Ink Pen Diva, LLC

Cover Design: Christopher Davis, Jr., Ascension Marketing

ISBN:978-0-9992902-1-7

DEDICATION

To my daughter Hannah Joy Harris, thank you for being my biggest inspiration. You were the reason for my pause that got me to the place of business ownership. When I got pregnant with you, I paused to see if I needed to make any real changes in business and in life. I made some major changes, restructuring where it was needed. That pause put me in position to sell my business two years later. What was a 20-year goal to sell my business happened two years earlier because you were born. Thank you for changing my life and my world.

TABLES OF CONTENTS

Acknowledgements

Foreword

Introduction

SHIFT INTO GEAR 1

SHIFT INTO GEAR 2

SHIFT INTO GEAR 3

SHIFT INTO GEAR 4

REVERSE SHIFT

SHIFT INTO GEAR 5

ACKNOWLEDGEMENTS

Special Thanks to God for birthing this book in my spirit.

My husband Houston Harris for your patience during this process, your love, and encouragement.

My mentors Kadenia Javis, Rosalind Chamberlain, and Lee Williams for your constant push, words of encouragement, and advice.

To all my friends, family, and supporters who have been there for me throughout this process.

Foreword by Kadenia Javis, MBA

After 20 years as an entrepreneur in the Accounting Industry, I can relate to so many chapters in this book. Although I am celebrating my 20th Anniversary of serving clients, 2020 will be our 10th year as a full- time, open year round practice. It was a solo venture for 12 years, as I worked full time in city, state, and federal agencies before making the transition to Full Time Business Owner. No two-week paycheck to rely on and no benefits, but I tell you the rewards of freedom, flexibility, and financial stability paid off. After completing my first Accounting class at Limestone College, I fell in love with the fact that I can help people change their lives financially with the right coaching and providing financial literacy to them when we prepare their taxes.

I wanted the taxpayers to know that if they were receiving a refund to not look at is as they have hit the jackpot. I invited them to take a look at investing, creating a small business, sowing into their kids future or their future for that day if and when they are given a pink slip from their job. The emergency fund is the first conversation that I have with my clients. We strategize on how we will save three-six months of reserve in case of a health, accident, job or life event change.

Author Joy McLaughlin-Harris has a similar journey as she too was an adjunct professor and worked full-time. What I like about Joy and her book is that we both experienced a similar roller coaster in our personal lives. It seems as though even though I was the child, I had outgrown the adults in the family when it came to the blueprint of normal business transactions.

It isn't impossible, but it is challenging to maximize your potential as a business owner   when you cannot dedicate the daytime hours to it.

Sure you can hire personnel if your budget allows it, but most often times when you are self-employed you do not have the capital to hire personnel. Also, they often are not there working side-by side to carry out your vision on a daily basis.

In reading, *Making the Shift from Good to Great* by Joy McLaughlin-Harris I too agree that there is a difference between being Self-Employed and Owning a Business. I have discovered that you are only self-employed if your business cannot run without you in it. If you have to close down to attend a funeral, go to a child's conference, or travel to a workshop you are just self-employed. However, if your business can employ people and still be open when you are away then you are actually a business owner. It took some coaching for me to realize this.

We live in a country where we are free to start a business any and every day. Most of us that are business owners began with a home based business which is great for beginners and minimizes cost. As we brand ourselves and the supply and demand becomes greater then we have to make a leap of faith to a brick and mortar. The reality is most people do not take us seriously when we work from home.

The key to make that change is be bold in this moment. As Joy says in the title of this book, it's time to make the shift from self-employed to business ownership.

Making

The **Shift** From

Self-Employed to

Business

Ownership

INTRODUCTION

From the Desk of the Author Joy L. McLaughlin-Harris

There are levels to, "business ownership." It does not happen overnight. There are tears, pain, loss, sacrifice, and suffering, but the freedom that you gain down the road is so worth the transition from self-employed to business ownership.

I have been in the beauty industry for almost 19 years and an entrepreneur for 20. I have operated and owned several beauty salons and businesses in that timeframe. I finally figured out how to work smarter and not harder, make money in my sleep, and really be able to enjoy life and not be a slave to work. This book will give you the tips, tools, resources, and techniques that helped me create six figures working part-time, retire from working behind the chair in the beauty salon, and become the business owner of my company and not just self-employed.

Shift Point: *"Trading time for money is not business ownership."* **Joyspeaks2u**

You will notice these shift points throughout the book. They are designed for you to shift your thinking.

I considered myself a business owner for a long time, until I really knew the true meaning. I was always taught when you start a company, you are considered a business owner which is true by identification, but not by the detailed definition. Being a business owner means you have to put systems and automation in place that run without you and have employees or independent contractors working for you. This book is designed to teach you how to make the shift from self-employed to business ownership.

Shift Point: *"If you can dream it, you can do it."* **Walt Disney**

SHIFT

INTO

GEAR

1

Chapter One

Mindset Shift

SHIFT POINT: "It is impossible to progress without change and those who do not change their minds cannot change anything." George Bernard Shaw

When learning how to drive a stick shift for the first time, I had to prepare my mind for it. Driving a stick shift requires more skill and understanding than operating a vehicle with an automatic transmission. I had no idea where to start, but once I was giving information on how to start. I kept rehearsing that information in my mind and started to gain a little more confidence that I could drive a stick shift. Once I changed my mindset about driving the stick shift, gathered information to help me be more confident, and visualized myself successfully driving, my fear was minimized. I got in the car and gave it a try. It did not go so well at first, but after practicing for a while, I finally had a successful drive. I was able to drive it without thinking so hard about messing up. It became natural and I got better at it over time.

Shift Point: *"Change your thoughts and you change your world."* **Norman Vincent Peale**

Making the transition from self-employed to business ownership begins in your mind first. You have to believe that you can be a business owner before you can conceive it. You have to envision the possibility of your business working and running without you or it will never become your reality. Just like learning to drive a stick shift, once I was given more information, I became more confident. Once I shifted my mind, I made the first step to get in the car and start the process to driving a stick shift.

SHIFT POINT: *"You must see beyond your present reality."* **Joyspeaks2u**

Positive thoughts determine the quality of life and provoke actions. Our actions are the manifestations of our thoughts. Whenever I coach clients, the first month of my program is dedicated to mind transformation.

Mind transformation is always month one because I have to see how they view money, life, and business in order for my time with them to be more effective. Mindset is defined as the fixed or established way people think that predetermines a person's responses and interpretation of a situation. Mindset is a collection of thoughts and beliefs. I grew up poor and never heard anything positive about money. When I became an adult, I operated from a poverty mentality.

A poverty mentality is a mindset about money that develops over time. My poverty mentality influenced my behavior, beliefs that opportunities are limited, money should not be spent, success does not exist, and I was designed to always struggle. I never believed that I could be the woman to make over $20,000 in one month, $20,000 in one day, and make six figures in one year. Yet I did all three because I was exposed to life-changing information and I worked daily to shift my mindset concerning how I viewed money, people, places, and things.

SHIFT POINT: *"The mind, once stretched by a new idea, never returns to its original dimensions."* **Ralph Waldo Emerson**

Once your mind has been exposed to certain information, it knows that information even if you revert back to old habits. Mind transformation takes discipline. Just like the body responds better to healthier food choices, your mind requires ongoing healthy visions, sounds, and motivation. Your mind is where transformation takes place.

"And be not conformed to this world: but be ye transformed by the renewing of your mind, that ye may prove what is good, and acceptable, and perfect, will of God." (Romans 12:2)

My process to transforming my mind came with me not watching TV for a year, speaking positive affirmations, meditation and allowing God to transform my thoughts concerning me. It was hard to conceptualize not watching TV for a year when I felt like I had personal relationships with the characters from my favorite shows like Good Times, Facts of Life, and The Jeffersons. I purposely put my TV on the other side of my room with the remotes next to it and put a piece of paper over the TV screen that read, "You have better things to do. Look at your bank account if you need a reminder." The sheet on my TV was a constant reminder to do something better with my time and thoughts. TV was cramping my social life and I needed to be out making connections and recruiting for new clients to take my business to the next level.

Somethings I notice within the first few weeks of not watching TV is that there was much more time in one day and so many other forms of stimulating and courageous entertainment in SC. I was much more productive and got into the best shape of my life. My body was not quite where I wanted it, but I was working hard to get there.

SHIFT ACTIVITY

What are you willing to give up or sacrifice for growth and a mindset shift?

_____

_____

_____

_____

_____

_____

_____

_____

_____

_____

_____

_____

_____

_____

_____

_____

_____

_____

_____

_____

_____

_____

_____

_____

_____

Who will be your accountability partners?
_____

_____

_____

_____

_____

_____

I fed my mind with constant motivation that I could and would be successful. I got mentors that held me accountable to do and be better daily. I worked on my attitude daily. This started with positive affirmations. An affirmation is the action of affirming something or being affirmed. I created a positive affirmation and read it daily until I truly believed what I was saying. I surrounded myself with positive notes, posts, and I turned my radio in my car into a library. Les Brown and John C Maxwell are some of my favorite authors and audio books I listen to daily.

My Affirmation for that season of my life:

Daily Affirmation

This is the Day the LORD has made,
I will rejoice and be glad in it,
Today will be a great day,
Today will be an awesome day,
The favor of God will rest upon me,
I am fearfully and wonderfully made,
I am a lender and not a borrower,
I am the head and not the tail,
I am above and not beneath,
I am everything that God says I am
Unique, Outstanding, Extraordinary, Chosen
The joy of the Lord is my strength,
And With God, All things are **POSSIBLE!**

"Death and life are in the power of the tongue: and they that love it shall eat the fruit thereof." (**Proverbs 18:21**)

SHIFT ASSIGNMENT

Let's create your affirmation:

_____

_____

_____

_____

_____

_____

_____

_____

_____

_____

_____

_____

_____

_____

_____

_____

_____

_____

_____

_____

_____

_____

_____

_____

_____

_____

_____

_____

_____

_____

_____

_____

_____

_____

_____

_____

_____

My affirmations became a daily habit for me when I woke up in the morning and I would pull from different lines of my affirmation and meditate on those words.

Meditation

By limiting my television watching, I found time to meditate, learn more about myself, and developed the best strategy ever to take my business to the next level. Meditation became a weekly, sometimes daily practice. Meditation is the act of practicing meditating, a written or spoken discourse expressing considered thoughts on a subject. I often meditated on the Word of God concerning me and just to be reminded that I was fearfully and wonderfully made, a royal priesthood, and a chosen nation. Sometimes a single quote, Scripture, or song would calm my mind, spirit, and soul.

Shift Point: *"Quiet the mind, and the soul will speak."*
Ma Jaya Sati Bhagavati

Meditation reduced my stress, improved my memory, and helped me to be more productive in business. My thoughts were more positive during the day and I was able to process information better. My cognitive potential was sharpened more and I was less frustrated in my mind when new business or life challenges came my way. I noticed a shift in my emotions towards people, places, and things. I often told others in my circle to try meditation and all reported back to me that the meditation made a difference in the flow of their day.

The executive director of Ford Motor Company takes the time to meditate daily. Bill Ford admitted in one of the Harvard Business Reviews he wrote, *"The practice of meditation helped him improve his productivity, but also to make decisions with compassion and kindness."* Russell Simmons wrote a piece detailing his perspective on meditation and encouraging new and experienced entrepreneurs alike to build the habit.

Both anecdotal and empirical evidence seem to suggest that regular time devoted to mindfulness and meditation can help you feel better, think well, and work better.

Chapter 2

Run Your Personal Finances like a Highly Successful Business

Shift Point: "Don't tell me what you value, show me your budget, and I'll tell you what you value. " Joe Biden

If the GPS does not have a starting point, it cannot properly guide you to find your destination. It's the same way with your finances. You want to be a successful business owner, but have no idea where you are in your personal finances. This is how you set yourself up for failure. There's going to be times on the journey even after creating the spending plan that things get off track, but having a spending plan better prepares you. Things come up, life happens, and family borrows money. There will be times where you will use your personal money for your business, but be sure to put business money in a business account and write yourself a check just to keep a tracking system and better position your finances.

Shift Point: *"One of the greatest disservices you do to a man is to lend him money that he can't pay back."* Jesse H. Jones

There are always the same family members who ask for money and forget you have a family of your own, bills, and other financial obligations. My new favorite word is, "No." I and my husband have put a number in place that we must keep in savings at all times and if we get below that number and someone needs something, we don't have it to give. If $5,000 is your number to have in your savings at all times, and once it hits $4,999 and someone calls to borrow money that you know is careless with their finances, you don't have it to give. You may not use this system or example, but be sure to put something in place to protect your personal finances. Often times we are building for five extra years because we are giving people bricks from our bank accounts. When we do this, it takes longer to see your vision and dreams come to past.

Shift Point: "An unwritten plan is impossible to follow." William V. Thompson

SHIFT ACTIVITY ... Review Your Financial Number (Personal Finances)

If you are self-employed and your money changes, put down your monthly average and not your highest month of income you have made

Inflows (any money coming) – Outflows (any money going out) = Your Financial #

Inflows	Outflows
Salary (Net)	Pay God
Income 1	Yourself
Income 2	Taxes

Income 3	Bills
Income 4	Mortgage/Rent
Income 5	Utilities
Income 6	Cable
Income 7	Internet
	Gas
	Car maintenance
	Car insurance
	Grocery
	Fast Food
	Loans
	Dog/Childcare
	Miscellaneous
	Personal
	Other
	Other
Total	

Financial Number_____ - _____ = _____

Researchers have pinpointed on average that millionaires have seven streams of income.

I often tell people my story of when I did this exercise for the first time and how my bank account was bleeding like the woman with the issue of blood. My number was negative, and I saw no way of coming out of this bloody mess.

Make sure that as you are creating this spending plan, you find the number that you must put in savings. The principles I follow are to pay God, yourself, and your bills. I recently added paying my taxes in because as business owners, you want to start paying taxes throughout the year. My new principle is pay God, myself, taxes, and my bills last.

A lot of people can't wrap their mind around paying themselves before bills. You have to get in the practice of saving to transition from self -employed to business ownership. When you don't have savings, everything becomes an emergency. If the tire burst, you will tap into whatever money you have, if anything, because you did not prioritize savings.

I pay my taxes because it helps me not to have to pay back so much money at the end of the year. And after experiencing my 1st lien on my credit for back taxes, a 50 point decrease in my credit score and paying high monthly payments to the IRS, I came up with a better system to pay my taxes. When you pay your taxes during the year, you save money. When you wait, the interest is more.

Saving money and cutting monthly expenses should be a constant goal. Since we've discussed credit, let's discuss some immediate habits you can put into place to help your savings grow, prepare for retirement, and increase your financial number.

I started my IRA, (Individual Retirement Account), when I was 18 years old. I was advised at that time to do a Roth IRA versus a traditional IRA. Both Roth and Traditional IRA's provide tax breaks. This was all new to me, but I knew I had to put something in place for retirement since I was not working for anyone else. Traditional IRA contributions are tax- deductible on both state and federal tax returns for the year you make the contributions; withdrawals in retirement are taxed at ordinary income tax rates. Roth IRAs provide no tax break for contributions, but earnings and withdrawals are generally tax-free.

I now understood why I was advised to do a Roth vs Traditional. I remember my banker asking me if I was going to purchase a home and of course my reply was, "yes." I used the money out of my Roth IRA to purchase my 1st home and it was not taxed for pulling out early.

Ways to Increase Your Financial Number

*Increase your dependents to get money during the year instead of a big tax refund at the end of the year

*Get a roommate

*Eat out less

*Get a car you can afford

*Get rid of cable

*Reduce cell phone bill

*Shop thrift stores for clothes

*Don't lend out money you can't afford to miss

Change happens when you move from where you are.
Mindsets, habits, and behaviors drive change.

SHIFT ACTIVITY

Identify three bad habits that can get in the way of
your financial goal becoming a reality. List those habits
and replace them with three good habits.

_____

_____

_____

_____

_____

_____

_____

_____

_____

_____

_____

_____

_____

Chapter 3

Credit Check

Shift Point: "Credit is a young man's capital."
Oscar Wilde

Knowing your credit is an important part of shifting from self-employment to business ownership. You can get a free report each year from annualcreditreport.com. These reports don't display your scores. You will have to pay a little extra to get your scores. Banks also have programs to check your score and there are other tracking systems to let you know if your score drops or increases. Credit Karma is one of the most popular sites today and it can be very beneficial to ensure you stay on top of what is on your report.

SHIFT ACTIVITY

Pull Your Credit Score (annualcreditreport.com)

Once you discover your credit score, you can start working on improving it. There are many companies that assist with credit repair, but there are a lot of things you can do on your own.

Eight tips to improve your credit score

*Pay your bills on time

*Work on paying off debt

*Pay more than the minimum balance

*Reduce your debt to income ratio

* Pay credit card bills down

* Be sure to dispute and get removed any incorrect items on your credit

* Have a good mix of debt

-Mortgage loan

-Bank credit cards

-Installment loan

-Retail

*Keep credit card debt below 30% monthly

When I first checked my credit score, it was a 514. I was 19 years old and already had several credit cards, my family had stuff on my credit already, and I had a personal loan. When my score was being pulled to get the cards and loans, I never asked what it was nor did I care at the time. I needed a car so I had to discover it. Once I found out about my 514 credit score, this was the reality check that I had bad credit. I was able to get a car, but the interest rate was 14%. I was excited to

have a car and at that time, I did not really understand interest rates and how they worked with credit. I later found out that my credit score impacted how much I paid for insurance, so I really got serious about working on my credit after hearing that.

I studied credit and sought help from my mentors on how to get my score increased. The first thing I was told to do was visit optoutprescreen.com and I ended up getting a 10 point increase. I was advised to get a secure card next and pay down my credit cards. I got 80 points by doing that within the first two months and from there, I kept reading and finding other ways to build my credit. Now that my score was better, I refinanced my 14% interest vehicle which gave me more money monthly that I applied to my debt. Better credit gives you better interest rates which can bring more money back into your household or business.

Within six months, I was at a 625. It felt like a 700 to me based on where I was. That was a 111 point increase and all I did was ask questions, read, and become better disciplined in my spending habits. It cost me a phone call, research, and a mentor.

If you can find programs that can assist with yours, it is worth the investment. Just make sure the company you are using is legitimate and can help you get results that you need. You can locate a credit counseling agency through the National Foundation for Credit Counseling. There was still more work to do with rebuilding my credit, but getting out of debt, increasing credit, and becoming better financially is not an overnight process.

Shift Point: *"There are no shortcuts when it comes to getting out of debt. "*Dave Ramsey

The one thing that I wish I knew when I first started my business or entrepreneurial journey was how to build business credit. I will talk more about this in the next book on building business credit. Building business credit will help you keep more of your personal money in the bank and really position you to shift from self-employment to business ownership from day one.

SHIFT ACTIVITY

What are you plans in the next 30-90 days to increase your credit score?

_____

_____

_____

_____

_____

_____

_____

_____

_____

_____

SHIFT INTO GEAR

2

Chapter 4

Self- Employed Worker

Shift Point: There's a way to do it better-find it."
Thomas Edison

After some experience driving a stick shift, you will be able to figure out when to shift into the next gear. It works the same in business, you will know when it's time to take things up a notch, reorganize, or create a better execution plan.

While self-employment is a great way to get your foot wet in the business world, it's much more crowded. Business ownership is waiting for you. According to an article written by Jennifer Good in March 3, 2016, 80% of small business in the United States is self-employment and 24% of business tends to fail in the first year and 48% won't make it pass the 2nd year. I believe that if more of these companies knew the power of business ownership over being self - employed, those numbers would be lower.

Sometimes the words self-employed and business owner are used interchangeably. Let's closely examine the difference. They are not closely related. They are not even cousins.

Self-employed is defined by relating to or designed for people working for themselves or owner of a business.

Self-employed is basically a job, the only difference is you do not have a boss. You are the boss and employee. Being self-employed is much better than working for someone. You can't get fired unless you fire yourself. You have more personal financial freedom than an employee. You get to do what you love and choose the people you work with. When you are self-employed, you do business as a sole proprietor, independent contractor or are in part-time business for them self.

Shift Point: "The problem with self-employment is that wealth is still achieved through income rather than equity." Louis Baraja

Despite the advantages of being self-employed, there are some inevitable risks. The biggest problem with being self-employed is over working. I can so relate to this in my 20 years of entrepreneurship. I only figured how to make the shift within the last five years. I wrote this book so you can learn from my mistakes and to lessen your learning curve so that it does not take you almost 20 years to become a business owner. You will not get holiday pay, sick pay, or any other employee benefit. Being self-employed is a different situation.

Shift Point: "Self- employed people don't own their business, their business owns them." Joyspeaks2u

My definition of self-employed is working countless hours daily and if I don't work, I don't eat because I have nothing in place to keep my finances flowing. It's working the 50, 60, 70 hour work week. It's the countless nights of limited sleep, or taking $5.00 and trying to figure out how to pay over $500 in bills. This was the story of my life throughout my late teen years, early 20s, and some of my 30s. Many self-employed people have a job and not a business.

Freelancers, independent local service providers, artists, e-commerce, and home-based businesses are examples of businesses or operations self-employed people might own. I knew there had to be a better way of life for me and being self-employed was just part of the transition to becoming a true business owner.

SHIFT ACTIVITY

If something happens to you or you have to take time off, is your business position to run without you?

_____

_____

_____

_____

If you answer, "Yes," congrats to you. Read on to increase your financial number and position yourself for greater financial success.

If you answer, "No," this book will really change your life and finances. Let's help you get to business ownership.

Chapter 5

Business Ownership

Shift Point: "Success consists of going from failure to failure without loss of enthusiasm." Winston Churchill

After working countless hours, having no real savings, and no vacations because my money would stop, I knew then that business ownership is not what I was experiencing. A true business had to be different. It was not the same as a job. A business is an organization of systems. It continues to work even when you are not working it. I knew that if I disappeared from my business for a week, struggling would be my reality. I had to learn how to get these systems going so I could transition to being a business owner.

According to Irs.gov, "Generally, you are self-employed if you carry on a trade or business as an independent contractor or sole proprietor, you are a member of a partnership that carries on a trade or business, or you in part time business for yourself. As a business owner, when others work for you, they must be identified as an independent contractor or employee." Many people like me start off self-employed and shift to becoming a business owner over time.

A business owner is seeking returns on their investment commensurate with the skill, capital and time invested. Business owners are looking for much more than wages. When you think like a business owner, you are thinking about leadership, development of capital, and management of the business.

Growing a business takes leadership, perseverance, and critical thinking. Leadership in business is the action of leading employees to achieve goals and have a clear vision. Strong leadership can help organizations reach goals and maximize productivity."

SHIFT POINT: "Growth is never by mere change; it is the result of forces working together." James Cash Penny, Founder of JCPENNEY

Perseverance is important because there's going to be days things get hard and you will want to give up. Perseverance is steadfastness in doing something despite difficulty or delay in achieving success. It is tenacity and persistence.

"I can do all things through him who gives me strength." (Philippians 4:13)

Critical thinking is essential in transitioning from self-employed to business ownership. Critical thinking helps you understand the logical connections between ideas, identify the relevance and importance of arguments, detect inconsistencies or mistakes in reasoning and make proper decisions. Critical thinking is the intellectually disciplined process of actively and skillfully conceptualizing, applying, analyzing, synthesizing, and evaluating information gathered from, or generated by observation, experience, reflection, reasoning, or communication, as a guide to belief or action.

When you are a business owner, you are building something that has value. You are creating an asset that you can later sell or pass to your children. You are getting to a place where you are working on your business instead of the day to day working *in* your business. Success is not only financial, but it also involves having time freedom and true balance.

Shift Point: Proverbs 13:22, "A good man leaves an inheritance to his children's children, but the sinner's wealth passeth to the godly."

Business owners invest in high level mentorship, outsources to free up time, and focus on very specific and target clients. Their focus is beyond just making enough to make ends meet. Business owners set aside time for creativity and innovation. So take a pause and look at your truth today. Are you self-employed or a business owner?

SHIFT ACTIVITY

Now that you have define the difference between self-employed and business ownership. Which one are you?

_____

_____

_____

_____

_____

_____

_____

_____

_____

_____

Let's keep shifting......

Chapter 6

Independent Contractor

Shift Point: *"Even if you're on the right track, you'll get run over in your mind."* -Author Unknown

I was a booth renter in a beauty salon for several years. I was considered self-employed because I was an independent contractor of the booth I was renting. I rented a space from the owner. I only made money doing hair and I was only working to pay bills at this time. I am sure a lot of you can relate to this. I barely made enough to pay the bills a lot of the times in the beginning of my journey. After learning that being an independent contractor was considered being self-employed, I knew I was in the wrong category.

An independent contractor is a person or entity contracted to perform work or provide services to another entity as a non-employee. As a result, independent contractors are responsible for their own taxes.

Independent contractors are 1099 workers. A 1099 employee is one that does not fall under normal employment classification rules. A contractor works under their own guidance. As a self-employed individual, you must pay Social Security and Medicare taxes. Since 1099-MISC income is not subject to employment-tax withholding, you are required to pay these taxes yourself. These taxes are calculated on a Schedule SE.

I didn't like the way things were going in the salon I was working in at the time, so I found another salon to work in. This next salon was not at all professional and I was ready for a change after two weeks of working there. I was tired of paying booth rent, so I began the process of opening my own salon. Keep in mind that I only made money doing hair at this time and had no real savings. This is when I finally decided to shift how I was doing things like I talked about in the earlier chapters by shifting my mindset and doing better with paying God, myself, taxes, and my bills.

"Bring the whole tithe into the storehouse, that there may be food in my house. Test me in this, says the Lord Almighty, and see if I will not throw open the floodgate of heaven and pour out blessings that there will not be room enough to store it." (Malachi 3:10)

I pitched the idea of owning my own business to my boyfriend Cory at the time. He was excited and on board, so we did it together and became business partners. I made great money doing hair so I took the money I made over the next few months and finally started saving it to open my business. Cory contributed his portion and three months later, we signed our 1st lease to start the road to business ownership.

Shift Point: "Don't open a business with a temporary person." Joyspeaks2u

I did it. Touch of Joy Beauty Salon was born. I was a business owner at 20 years old. I was excited and afraid at the same time. My relationship with Cory became very shaky and we no longer had a relationship, we were only business partners. We budget enough money to get everything done and had a little left in savings. What we did not budget was the light bill deposit that was almost $1,000.

I was out of money before the doors opened and Cory was no longer contributing anything. Not even two months in and I was a solo owner with Cory as my partner in name only. I managed to get the salon open and get some girls working in the salon within three months. I was barely making it financially, but I kept pushing. The relationship was over with Cory and he wanted his money back. That's another book.

I was getting back on track financially and paying God and my bills. I was still struggling to pay my taxes and myself, but I was making an effort and doing better.

With a start-up business, you have to be aggressive in paying yourself. Minimize your over head in order to decrease the amount of capital you needed on a monthly basis. By reducing overhead, your net loss will decrease or net profit will increase. I had to find someone that knew about business fast to talk to, mentor me, or just give me some direction.

SHIFT ACTIVITY

What ways can you decrease overhead expenses in your business?

_____

_____

_____

_____

_____

_____

_____

_____

_____

_____

_____

_____

_____

SHIFT

INTO

GEAR

3

Chapter 7

Multiple Streams of Income

Shift Point: "Never depend on a single income."
Warren Buffett

It takes dedication and research, but the opportunities are out there for you to create more income in your business and personal finances. It is no longer a luxury to create more income, but a necessity with the constant increases on life. Creating multiple streams of income allows you to diversify the various cash flow sources that are coming in.

SHIFT Point: "Whenever you start a business, have more than one way that produces money financially."
Joyspeaks2u

I was in over my head. I started to accumulate so much debt with my salon and personal finances. I no longer had a full team of girls and booth rent was the only income I had coming in outside of my money from doing hair. I was becoming depressed, overwhelmed, and I emotionally disconnected from everything. I knew the power of prayer and this season of struggle pushed me to prayer like never before. I knew a major shift was going to have to take place, a miracle, and a break through. I was led to the story about Sarah and Abraham in the Bible in Genesis 21.

I learned from this story that I was giving birth to Ishmael and not Isaac. If you go back and read the story, Isaac was the child of promise, but because Sarah lacked faith, she told her husband to sleep with the maidservant and she became pregnant and Ishmael was born. Ishmael had to be taken care of like any child. My salon had to be taken care of as well, but my faith didn't develop enough for me to give birth to Isaac, so the load was more stressful than it had to be. In me not waiting, I still ended up developing the faith I needed in that season.

That season also taught me that I had an anxiety issues.

Shift Point: "*Do not be anxious about anything, but in every situation, by prayer and petition, with thanksgiving, present your request to God.*"
(*Philippians 4:6*)

My anxiety got the best of me. Trying to take on too much at one time, not counting the real costs, and not letting my savings grow more. Of course, my savings, bank account, and everything with $ sign connected to it was in the red at this time.

Shift Point: "Have six months of savings for personal bills before starting a business." Joyspeaks2u

Shift Point: *"Consider it pure Joy, my brothers and sisters whenever you face trials of many kinds, because you know the testing of your faith produces perseverance." (James 1:2)*

Shift Point:

"And we know All things work together for the good of those that love the Lord." (Romans 8:28)

I downsized my salon and rented a space in another building that was more affordable.

Shift Point: "What appears to be a step down is a step up." Joyspeaks2u

It was about three months in at the new location and I was seeing a complete turn- around in my finances. I had more money in the bank because I did not have all the overhead from both salons. I created more ways to make money. I started to retail products so I could have a source of income.

SHIFT ACTIVITY

List all the ways your business produces money. If you only have one way, this is where you create other ways

to make money. Create a plan and timeline of execution.

Simple Execution Plan

Product you want to sell (T-Shirts) with your logo design

Locate vendor that sells shirts, research costs

Find a designer for your shirt and cost it will take to make it a reality

Pay for design

Action Timeline

T-Shirt	Jan.	Feb.	Mar.
	Price Shirts	Shirt Design paid	Market on social media
	Find designer/cost	Print 1st set	Wear shirt daily

_____

_____

_____

_____

_____

_____

_____

_____

_____

_____

_____

_____

_____

_____

_____

_____

_____

_____

_____

_____

_____

_____

_____

_____

Shift Point: "It's not enough just to write down ideas without a plan of action in place." Joyspeaks2u

One of my income streams in the salon was retailing products. I did not always retail products, but I took a class that taught me skills to maximize retail sales and I increased my income by $20,000 in the 1st year.

Shift Point: "One change can do a lot for your finances in the business world." Joyspeaks2u

I use the T-shirt example because that was the 1st product I created with my brand on it. I was amazed at the amount of people that wanted a T-Shirt that represented my brand. I was selling 10 shirts minimum each month when I first started at $10 and making an additional $100 monthly with my shirts which totaled $1200 yearly. Of course, there were months when I made more. But two income sources gave me a total of $21,200 in one year. Not bad for a girl in her early 20s.

One thing I would encourage you to do is make sure what you create works with your business. For example if you own a gym, you might start selling shakes. If you have a retail shop and you sell shoes, you might look into custom shoes for your clients. This is just to name a few. Go back and review your new income sources to make sure you are not all over the place. All over the place is selling chicken dinners in the salon because you are just trying to make ends meet.

Everything in this book is designed to help you transition from self-employed to business ownership. I still was working behind the chair in the hair salon because that's how I was making the bulk of my money. I was still not at a point where if I took a vacation, I would be ok. I was not producing enough yet.

Chapter 8

Making Money in Your Sleep

Shift Point: *"To get rich, you have to be making money while you're asleep."* **David Bailey**

Once I discovered the cashflow quadrant in the book *Rich Dad, Poor Dad* by my book mentor Robert Kiyosaki, it was my reality check that I was self-employed again and not a business owner. The cashflow quadrant explains the various career paths and explains our tax system structure. E and S quadrants are on the left side and B and I quadrants on the right. The diagram 8.1 on the next page better explains the cashflow quadrant.

I wanted to be a business owner and own property. I wanted to be in a position to leave money for my family if something ever happened to me and position myself for financial freedom.

Now that I am a mother and wife, I am more motivated to see that my family is taken care of if something happens to me. I have experienced the left side of the cashflow quadrant and made a decision that it was not for me. I teach in my financial literacy classes that if you are on the left side and work for someone, you

want to get to a point where your stable income (JOB) creates assets and your assets pays your bills and creates your lifestyle. This helps you be in position if your job decides one day to FIRE you. You have put something in place to protect yourself and family.

8.1 Cash Flow Quadrant

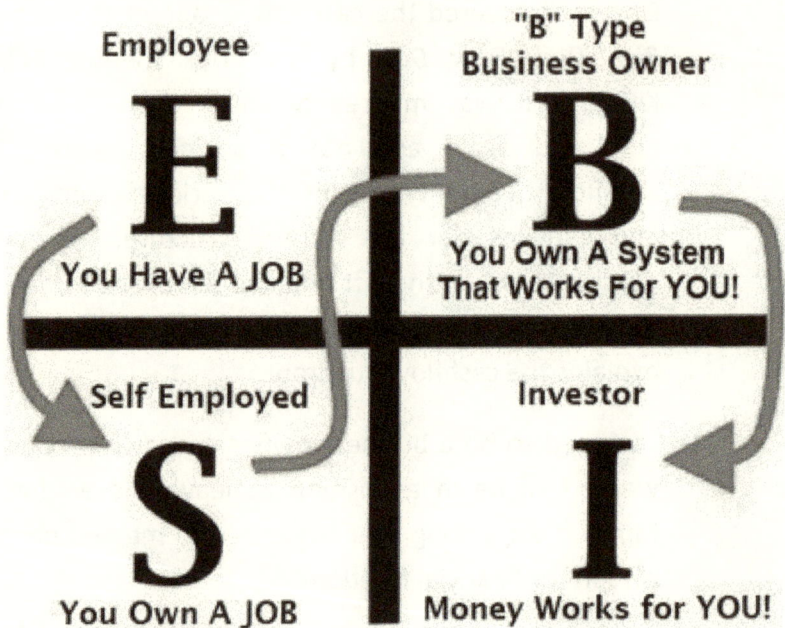

Cash Flow Quadrant

Employee- You get paid for your time. You are trading hours for dollars. You're working for someone else, and in return they give you a paycheck.

Self-employed- People work for themselves, they often trade their hours for dollars. Or perhaps they work for a fee or commission.

Business owner- You own a system and people work for you.

Investors- Money works for you. This is where you truly have passive income. Investments like stocks, bonds, and real estate. It can also be things like trademarks, copyrights, and royalties.

Active income is on the left side. You are trading time for money and in order to make money, you must be performing something. Passive income is on the right side and you do not have to be present to generate income. You are literally making money while you sleep.

Shift Point: "If you don't find a way to make money in your sleep, you will work until you die." Warren Buffett

I remember the first time I experienced making money in my sleep. I know I wanted to experience that feeling daily and bring others on board with me.

If your company is a service-based company, you have to come up with a product or link your business to an existing system or company.

For example if you are a makeup artist and you don't have your own makeup line or know where to start, link up with a home-based business where you can get discounted products and make money while recruiting, selling products, and more.

Passive income is you doing something one time and continually getting paid. This book you are reading Is another way for me to make money in my sleep, create royalties, and create more income. One product can produce multiple ways to make money. When I talked about having seven income streams, it does not have to be seven different things. It can be one product that provides several income streams.

There are several ways to make money in your sleep, but these are some I used, currently starting, or friends have used and created great success stories.

7 Ways to Make Money in Your Sleep

*Affiliate marketing - If you already have an audience, affiliate marketing can really be beneficial. Clickbank is a great platform.

*Real Estate Rentals is a popular way to gain passive income. People are always going to need a place to live.

*Blogging- Create information about your niches and sell product in the same place.

*Online Courses- Kajabi, Teachable, and Udemy are places you can build online courses. Once you create them, you just have to update content to keep it relevant.

*Drop Shipping-Ecommerce is exploding. As a store owner, you never have to touch the products. Warehouse will ship and deliver in your name. You can build your own store through shopify and amazon FBA store.

*EBooks 60-80 pages long are a great spot for books, but you can write a little less or more. You can use Amazon, but your own platform is even better.

*Webinars- automated webinars are a great way to generate passive income

SHIFT POINT: Our tax system is designed to favor large businesses and investors. Joyspeaks2u

SHIFT ACTIVITY

Name one additional way you will make money in your sleep and list your plan to accomplish this new stream of income.

_____

_____

_____

_____

_____

_____

_____

_____

_____

_____

_____

_____

_____

_____

_____

_____

_____

_____

_____

_____

_____

**SHIFT POINT: "The best way to build wealth is to turn
your active income into multiple passive incomes."
Joyspeaks2u**

Optimization is the practice of increasing the quantity and quality traffic to your website through organic search engine results.

Another recent thing I started doing was purchasing sponsorship ads through Facebook and Instagram to expand my reach. Sponsor Ads have been beneficial in reaching other markets and have opened the door to new connections and revenue increase. I save money doing this form of marketing. Most social media advertising is less expensive than traditional advertising, so you do not have to spend a lot of money to increase your audience, reach people, and grow your business.

I finally started blogging, maximizing my YouTube channel, and more. I will talk more about the power of blogging, YouTube, and Amazon marketing in my next book. It's not enough to have social media and people are not engaged or you don't know how it's benefiting you.

SHIFT ACTIVITY

List your current social media sites and how you are maximizing social media or list your plan to start maximizing social media.

_____

_____

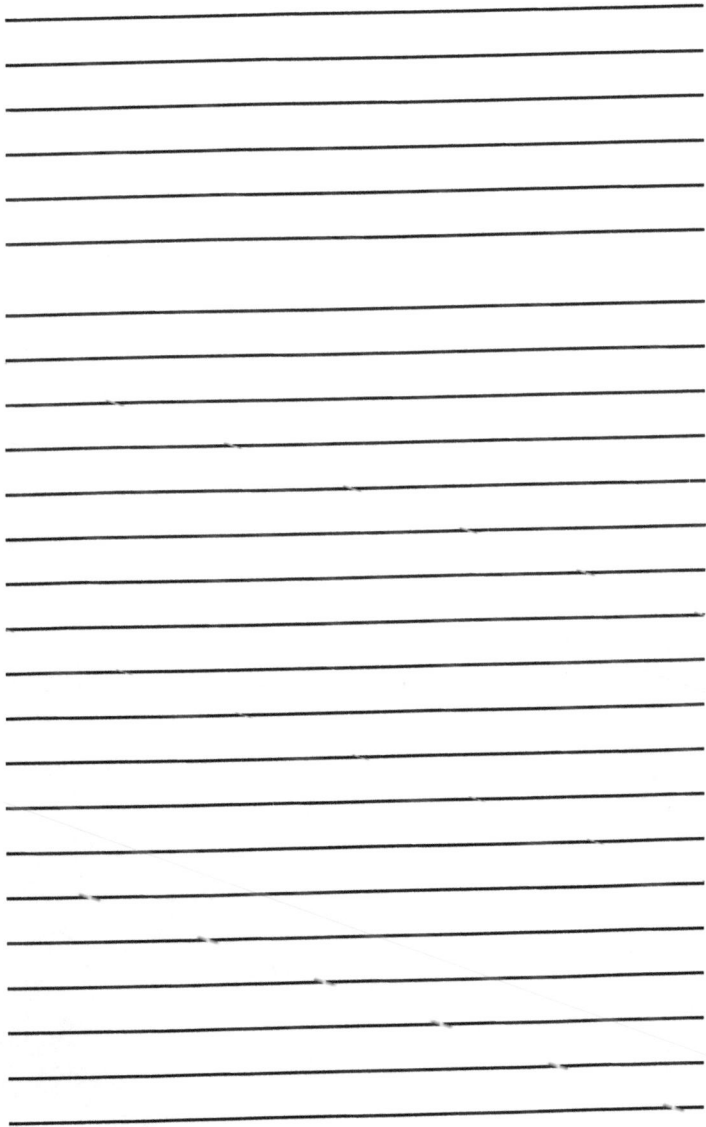

CHAPTER 10

POWER of FOLLOW-UP

Shift Point: "The follow-up can seal the deal."Joyspeaks2u

It's always amazing to me how many business owners I talk to that do not follow-up with potential clients. I can think of several times over the last 12 months that I reached out to inquire about using a business and never received a call or an e-mail back. I didn't even get an automated response. In each of these situations, I was interested in the product or service offered by the business owner.

We want to avoid being annoying or risk being rejected. Well in business, you have to get over being rejected. It happens to the best of us. Learning how to keep things short and sweet in following up helps you not come off annoying or aggravating. A simple e-mail after you sent a proposal, a thank you card after you met someone who interests you, or a voice message is all it takes sometimes to seal a deal.

When sending a quote or proposal, let your customers know when you will be following up with them and be sure to follow-up. It can say something simple like, "Please let me know which quote you decided to go with and if you have any questions.

I wear my shirts and read my books whenever I travel out of state as a way to promote my brand and I walk away every trip with a new booking or products sold. Just wearing a shirt to the airport, supermarket, or anywhere can result in a potential new client or sale.

Have an elevator pitch ready when someone asks you about your company. An elevator pitch is a script description of an idea, product, company, or oneself that explains the concept in a way such that any listener can understand it in a short period of time. The name comes from the notion that the speech should be delivered in a short time period of an elevator ride.

Shift Point: *"If you can't explain it, you don't understand it."* **Joyspeaks2u**

When people see me wear my shirt or just ask about my business, my elevator speech is, "Touch of Joy helps entrepreneurs start their business on a firm foundation, maximize revenues, make money in their sleep, and assist companies with organizational leadership and development. Do you know anyone that could use these services?" Over 50 % of the time, I get a new client from my follow-up from my elevator pitch.

If you get a card from the person you said an elevator pitch to or a recommendation, be sure to follow-up.

Not only in the case of an elevator speech, follow-up with all potential clients.

The power of follow-up can make or break a deal. This follow-up can result in a potential client, another referral, and increased sales. Most people would contact someone once and wait for that person to get back with them. That is the wrong approach. Most business owners or potential clients are busy with the day-to- day hustle and bustle of life.

I normally try to send a thank you card by mail within a week of meeting the person or use the power of social media and send a thank you card saying, "Thanks for sharing your card or contact information with me. I am looking forward to hearing from you or connecting with you soon." If it's another business owner and I want to learn more about what they do, I might suggest meeting for coffee once they reply to the e-mail. If it's a potential client, I am going to try to schedule a consultation to see if my services may be a good fit for them once they reply. Follow-up emails or messaging is a way to establish relationship, build trust and understanding. The goal in the end is to provide superior service, but close the deal.

If I don't get a response back, I might reach back a few times if I had no prior connection or relationship with the person, but double the amount of times I reach back out if I had a prior connection with the person.

SHIFT ASSIGNMENT

Let's Create an Elevator Pitch or Write down your current elevator pitch.

Follow these steps to craft a good elevator speech

*Identify your goal

*Explain what you do

*Identify your usp (unique selling pitch) What makes your organization unique

*Engage with a question

*Put it all together

*Practice

Try to stay within 20-30 secs (1 floor ride on the elevator)

_____

_____

_____

_____

_____

_____

_____

Chapter 11

Power of Mentorship

Shift Point: "A mentor is someone who allows you to see hope inside of you." Oprah Winfrey

I started reading books by the late Dr. Myles Munroe, Suze Orman, Dave Ramsey, and John C Maxwell. I only had two major business mentors at this time, but book mentors were just as powerful. Most successful entrepreneurs credit mentors when asked about the trajectories of their business.

I am often asked how to find a mentor. I tell people to search authors that are considered experts in their subject area and start there. When seeking any mentor, look to a person you admire or look up to. My two business mentors came through a networking marketing business I was a part of. I admired them and when an opportunity came for me to meet them face to face, I popped the question, "Will you become my mentor?" They both said how they admired my ambition and were honored to take me on as a mentee. It's not always that easy, but it's worth a try. I did have prior contact with them by phone or e-mail because I invested in a program or book so they both were familiar with me. Prayer can help lead you to the right person. There are countless organizations that provide mentorship. Tap into mentorship and reap all the benefits that come with it.

I started to really develop a passion for financial literacy and I wanted to help everyone learn how to make their money grow and work for them, but I was still trying to figure it out myself.

In the process of reading, the word assets became my new favorite term. Assets are things that make you money like real estate, stock market, and business ownership. You see why assets became my new favorite word? I was already transitioning to business owner so now I needed to tap into real estate, stock market, and other income streams to take my personal and business finances to the next level.

I joined an investment group for young people under 30 shortly after my conversation with my mentor Victor and learning more about the power of having assets. I was so excited about this investing group because this is where I purchased my 1st piece of real estate. When they told me what it was going to take to join the group financially because it was already six months old, I had the money needed to join the group. I finally had a savings and a credit card in good standing.

I was learning the power of leverage. Leverage is the use of various financial instruments or borrowed capital, such as margin, to increase the potential return of an investment. I was now experiencing the right side of the cashflow quadrant and knew this was my open door to building wealth and fully transitioning from self- employed to business ownership.

Shortly after joining the investment group, the group had a building they wanted to turn into a salon. They looked to me. My 1st salon was doing well so I opened a 2nd location. I was about 23 years of age and now owned two salons. My investors were my investing group so I was winning double.

Touch of Joy Braids and More was open. I wish I had pictures because it was a total transformation and we got it filled in no time. The area wasn't the best, so pricing was not what I normally would charge for booth rent compared to my other salon. The mindset of the workers was just like the area. It was challenging to get quality girls.

Not only was it a challenge getting quality workers, but customers in a specific target or market or area behave different. I went to the shop to work to make sure it stayed active and open when we had a season with only a few workers and the walk in traffic was very different.

Shift Point: "You can't have a poverty mentality and expect to grow in your finances." Joyspeaks2u

I did not do my due diligence and conduct detailed research for this area. To be successful in business, you have to find a gap in the market to exploit. Your aim should always be to stand out. The most powerful tool to do this would be research.

Shift Point: "Be sure to do your research before opening a business." Joyspeaks2u

I was more excited about having a 2nd salon more than anything.

SHIFT ACTIVITY

List your current mentors and how they have been an impact to your business and life?

_____

_____

_____

_____

_____

_____

_____

_____

_____

_____

_____

_____

_____

_____

_____

_____

_____

_____

_____

_____

_____

_____

_____

_____

_____

_____

_____

_____

_____

_____

_____

_____

_____

If you do not have any mentors, decide who you want to be your mentor and take action steps to see if that person or people will become your mentors.

Let's keep shifting....

Chapter 12

Do Your Research

Shift Point: *"Research is creating new knowledge."*
Neil Armstrong

Research lets you know the type of money people make in the area, how businesses are doing, and the price point you can charge. I did not look at any of these numbers at all. You need to size up the competition and know who else is doing what you plan to do, define your target market, and licensing and legal issues. Research will save you money further down the line so it is important not to skip this step. It's ok to go back and do research once the business has started and make the changes needed for your business to go and grow to business ownership.

Market analysis research involves a systematic review of the area you are looking into and your customer base. Having a better understanding of your market will help you create a better business strategy. Market research will also provide you with better understanding with competition in the same area.

Here some simple thing you can do before opening any business. A simple SWOT analysis is used to do these yearly, but now I do them monthly in my business.

When moving from self-employed to business ownership, it's important to do things more often.

SWOT analysis

S- Strengths

*Things your company does well

*Qualities that separate you from your competitors

*Internal resources such as skilled knowledgeable staff

*Tangible assets such as intellectual property, capital, proprietary technologies

W- Weakness

*Things your company lacks

*Resource limitations

Unclear unique selling proposition

*Things your competitor does better than you

O- Opportunities

*Few competitors in your area

*Press/media coverage for your company

*Emerging need for your product or service

*Few competitors in your area

T- Threats

Emerging competitors

*Changing regulatory environment

*Negative press/media coverage

*Changing customers attitude towards your company

Word stream

Benefit of SWOT

SWOT analysis can aim to evaluate the balance between the internal resources and capabilities of a company and external possibilities and threats.

A SWOT analysis can help you identify and understand key issues that could impact your business. It may not necessarily offer solutions but you can build solutions for what you discover.

SHIFT ASSIGNMENT

Create Your SWOT Analysis

STRENGTHS

_____

_____

_____

_____

_____

_____

_____

_____

_____

_____

_____

_____

_____

_____

WEAKNESS

_____

_____

_____

_____

_____

_____

_____

_____

_____

_____

_____

_____

_____

OPPORTUNITIES

_____

_____

_____

_____

_____

_____

_____

_____

_____

_____

_____

_____

_____

_____

THREATS

_____

_____

_____

_____

_____

_____

_____

_____

_____

Now build from your strengths and opportunity, hire your weakness, and now that you are aware of your threats, make decisions that will help you stand above the rest. SWOT analysis were good when starting a business with the way business change from day to day, I started doing a SWOT analysis quarterly and eventually switched to monthly.

Once I went back and did some research on the area, instead of offering lots of different services, we specialized in braids and renamed the salon Touch of Joy Braid Salon. This worked well because the salon was located near college campus. Our target market and prices were comfortable for college students and the people that live on that area.

SHIFT POINT: "Research is formalized curiosity. It is poking and prying with a purpose." Zora Neale Hurst.

REVERSE

GEAR

Chapter 13

Let's Talk Documentation

SHIFT POINT: "Taking a few steps back can position you to take several steps forward." Joyspeaks2u

Once you have the vehicle in reverse gear, it is time to drive backwards. I know you are wondering why I have you going backwards when the objective is to shift from self-employed to business ownership. I see this step in shifting gears as part of the evolution and refinement we all go through and am an essential part of growth into our true potential of becoming a business ownership.

When transitioning from self-employed to business ownership, you have to make sure you have great policies, procedures, and protection. Once you have the vehicle in reverse gear, it's time to drive backwards. Once you back into the park and take a look back at your documentation to make sure everything is polish and if any documents needed to be added as you make the shift. You can be better prepared when you take off to go to the next level. As a business owner, you face a variety of risks, especially when you begin to work with clients and hire staff.

The other thing I find when working with business is they never took the time to decide if they want to sell business, leave for family, or just phase out. This is something that should be considered from day one or if you experience a change in family size or life. You should have documentation in place that makes this process easier.

An operational plan is a must. I have a seminar that I deliver titled, "Business in a Binder." Someone should be able to open the binder and have the written information they need to run your company. This takes time to build, but it is one of the most valuable binders your company would offer. This binder is very detailed and filled with all your documents, and training information.. Some things you can find in your business in a binder are the following: Passwords and passcodes, instructions on how to run your systems and day to day operations, training documents, code of ethics, and policies and procedures.

Some forms everyone should make sure they have in place are confidentiality, code of ethics, and tax forms. Businesses are required by law to file certain forms for all their employees. These include forms mandated by the Internal Revenue Service and U.S. immigration office: an Employee Eligibility Verification form, Form I-9; a W-4 Wage and Tax Statement and a federal employee withholding allowance certificate or form W-4. I am not a tax attorney or accountant, but be sure to have one on your team.

Other important forms are employee handbooks, workplace safety measures, and financial forms. A lot

of these forms can be combined to create an employee handbook for orientation.

A lot of people decided not to work for me because I had so many forms for them to complete. My forms grew as my business did because more was required from me and my business had more people. Having protection documentation in place can save you later.

My later was when I got sued for the first time. My partner at the time was no longer a partner and wanted to be paid back for money that was put in. Because he did not start off as an investor and the paperwork was not structured that way, the judge did not order me to pay him back.

Shift Point: *"Good business owners are not exempt from getting sued."* **Joyspeaks2u**

I did get all my contracts that I use to rent out my individual suites updated. There were things that were not included in the original contract that need to be added. I just waited until it was time for contract renewal or new girls started to use the new contract agreement.

Contracts provide businesses and individuals with a legal document stating the expectations of both parties and how negative situations can be resolved. Contracts are legally enforced in a court of law. Because of the contract agreements I had in place when I went to court, that protected me from paying money out of pocket based on how the documentation was written and presented in court. Below are 8 things that make a business agreement and contract solid.

*Get it in writing- A written agreement is less risky than an oral agreement.

*KISS (Keep it simple stupid)- Make sure sentences are short, clear, and straight to the point. KISS was a designed principle noted in U.S. Navy in 1960. The KISS principle states that most systems work best if they are kept simple rather than more complicated.

*Identify each party correctly- Make sure each person is clear on their role in regards to the contract. Make sure you have the correct legal names.

*Spell out all the details- Spell out the rights and obligations of everything.

*Specify payment obligations- Make sure to less amounts, due dates, and if late fees will be attached if not paid on time.

*What happens if the contract is terminated- Outline the details of what's required if contract is terminated on both sides.

* Pick a state where contract will be govern- If parties are located in different state, you choose one state laws.

*Keep it confidential

Based on where you are at in business or your financial goals, this might be a time to see if you need an entity change. This is not the case for everyone, but some businesses can benefit if they switch to a C or S Corporation. As your income from your LLC increases or other business structure you may have, the self-employment tax increase. You earn more, you pay more, but your contribution to your retirement account does not change.

This is where converting the LLC to an S Corp has advantages. You are an employee and shareholder. As an employee, your income is subjected to all the taxes you would normally see on a paystub, however as a shareholder or investor, you are simply getting a return on your investment like a dividend or distribution in S Corp world terms.

Some of the reasons to switch to C corporations could mean lower overall federal income tax rates, potentially more flexible fringe benefits, and special gain exclusion for some C corporations.

I am sure there lots of other documentation, switches, or paperwork upgrades that I didn't mention, but these are a few I found very important in my business journey and have in place before hiring anyone. Business owners deal with liabilities every day and having documentation in place can help reduce some of that liability. Make sure all forms are created and reviewed by a professional attorney and consult with a tax advisor on best structure for your financial increase in business and overall goals.

SHIFT ACTIVITY

What current documentation do you have in place that needs to be upgraded or new documentation that need to be put in place?

_____

_____

_____

_____

_____

_____

_____

_____

_____

_____

_____

Chapter 14

Trademarks

Shift Point: "*A great trademark is appropriate, dynamic, distinctive, memorable, and unique.*" Primo Angeli

A trademark is a brand name. A trademark can be word, symbol, device, or product. The trademark is used to identify the goods and services of one business over another and to indicate the source of goods and services.

People often ask if trademarks are necessary and I tell them, "yes" if you have a product, slogan, or brand symbol you don't want anyone to steal. It protects your investment, products, and brand. If at this point in business you have not trademarked and you are planning to transition from self-employed to business ownership. To register a trademark, go to U.S. Patent and Trademark office website at www.uspto.gov. Make sure someone else has not registered the name by doing Trademark Electronic Search System database. This is a federal trademark registration and it extends your name nationwide and offers other important advantages. It normally costs $275 or more for each class of goods and services you want to protect. You can do a state registration and the cost is normally between $100-$200.

You normally see trademark symbols subscript TM or SM or the letter R in the circle and actually don't know that they are all different. The TM (trademark) or SM (service mark) designation is used to alert the public that you are claiming proprietary trademark rights in a particular mark. You are free to use it whether you file a trademark application with the U.S. Patent and Trademark Office or not. It is reserved for all unregistered marks.

The letter R in the circle is the federal registration symbol. It may only be used on the marks that have been registered with U.S. Patent and Trademark Office and only for good and services listed in the federal registration. Unlike the TM or SM, use of this symbol is regulated by federal law.

Once your paperwork is submitted for trademark, it normally takes about three months from filing the application to receiving a response. The total application time can be from six months to a year. You are reminded throughout this book that it's a process for everything.

Shift Point: "Don't rush the process." Joyspeaks2u

The term of federal trademarks is 10 years, with 10 year renewal term. After 5-6 years, you do have to file an affidavit to let the USPTO know the trademark is still being used.

Chapter 15

Create a Team

Shift Point: "No one can be good at everything."
Joyspeaks2u

A greater acceleration comes with shifting into gear 5. You are driving at 40mph or more because you are not the only person driving, you have help. Everyone can't drive a stick shift, but having people on your team keeps you from teaching every new person how to drive. You have now delegated responsibilities to others on the team. This was the 1st lesson I learned when you have a big vision.

Shift Point: "You cannot do BIG vision solo."
Joyspeaks2u

The path from being self-employed to a business owner is paved with great teams. Great teams put you in a position to delegate and take some of the work off of you.

The first thing I always hear from people is I can't afford an assistant or to hire a team. I learned fast that if you get the right team, in the end, you will produce more

Shift Point: "Incredible things in the business world are never made by a single person, but by a team."
Steve Jobs

I am sure I am not the only one who has been the five people on your own team. When you 1st start, you are the assistant, social media person, and accountant. However, you get to a place where you get so busy and even overwhelmed, you may forget to respond to an e-mail. This could create bad business reviews and missed money.

Shift Point: "Responding to messages is very important in entrepreneurship."

The social media world has taken a turn. There's so much available to you for free. These systems can be the beginning of TEAM BUILDING.

My 1st team players name was Hootsuite. I talked about this earlier in the social media chapter. It is not a physical person, but a social media system that I could use to automate my posts and help me create an active social media page when I was away from my computer. Putting this one system in place helped me produce more money.

My next team player was a personal assistant. When my workload increased, I could no longer sit down and create the posts for HOOTSUITE because it was taking time from me creating money producing activity so I paid her to do it. She had more time, so she took my marketing to another level. She made my posts look more polished. One of my weaknesses in the SWOT analysis earlier was social media.

I had to hire a receptionist, media team, marketing team, and other employees to make my business more successful. Some work directly for the company and others were independent contractors.

When looking to hire people, remember that every person on the team is a brand ambassador. Hire and set the right tone and make sure everyone on your team knows how you operate, what you stand for, and the kind of customer experience you plan to deliver. Your team is a reflection of your business and your business is you.

SHIFT POINT: "The first impression could be the last."
Joyspeaks2u

Dan Sullivan, author of *The Laws of Lifetime Growth*, came up with the KASH acronym to indicate what you should look for in a team.

Knowledge

Ability

Skills

Habits

You can train people in knowledge and skills, but it's hard to train habits and difficult to change abilities. Ability is tied to your unique gift.

The proof of if your team is great or working for you is if you are getting positive results that in return increases revenue and allows you to focus on other task for company success and growth.

Shift Point: "Hire your weaknesses."Joyspeaks2u

My personal assistant answers calls, responds to e-mails, and schedules my posts. She was also responsible for attending events to pass out my cards and get my business in front of new people and potential clients.

I was making more money and being more effective so I had to now learn to manage my funds at another level. Hiring an assistant gave me free time from doing administration work and I was able to shift my energy to other money producing activities.

Shift Point: "Learn money management and money discipline before you step into making more money." Joyspeaks2u

Do the normal background checks, application process, and in person interviews for your business and pick the best fit for your team.

I created my ideal team before I had a team. I knew I was going to need a personal assistant, marketing person and other employees that would have different roles and responsibilities.

One thing that I always did was celebrate my team efforts, special events, and just made sure that they felt appreciated. I did holiday gifts as well. Thank you notes or hand written notes always work well and the cost in inexpensive. I knew they all liked coffee so I would get $5 gift cards and leave a note with the gift card that said, "Have a cup of coffee on me." It wasn't real expensive stuff, but just creative gifts to let them know I appreciate them for believing in me, my dream, and vision.

There are benefits to recognizing and celebrating your team. Team members feel appreciated and it reinforces the meaning of one's hard work. Recognizing individual and team achievement helps build a sense of identity and solidarity for the entire team. Be sure to stop and celebrate. Don't just celebrate reaching the financial goal but celebrate getting the contract submitted.

SHIFT ACTIVITY

Let's create your ideal team with their roles and responsibilities:

Chapter 16

Creating Systems

Shift Point: "Systems enhance fluidity, productivity, and work quality."

Being an entrepreneur and business owner is a lifestyle. Putting systems in place is one way to work smarter and not harder. Let the systems work for you.

I meet business owners every day that have no system in place that runs without them or helps them work smarter and not harder. A system is a way of making functions automatic. A system simplifies your workload and allows you to become more efficient. A lot of business owners just work, produce, pay bills and have no idea how much money is being made or left if anything, at the end of the month. That sounds a lot like a self-employed person than business owner to me. If they don't work, they have nothing in place for someone else to run the business or money to keep the business going. Systems help create order, simplify life, and free up time.

Shift Point: "If you have to do everything yourself, you don't own a business, but a job." Joyspeaks2u

Life happens to the best of us, but if you have systems in place for your business, savings, and multiple streams of income in place that help you make money in your sleep. Systems play a significant role in building a company and serve as essential building blocks.

When people follow a set of steps, a process, and procedures, that is a system. More often than not, systems involve people using similar tools or software. A system can be assembled in a factory. You create systems that work for productivity and growth for your company. I can write an entire book on systems, but here are five systems that are essential for all businesses.

Communication System

A Communication System is a way that leadership and employees communicate and make sure that the expectation, mission, and vision are clear. A lot of people still use the old fashion way and send e-mails. E-mails alone can take up a large part of your day. Put a schedule in place to check e-mails, write, and file them.

SLACK is a recent tool I discovered that allows you to get those conversations out of e-mail and into a place that's searchable and much easier to get things done with the employees on their team. An effective communication system can help foster good working relationships and that alone can increase efficiency and morale.

Hiring System

It's important to have a system in place for people to know you are seeking new employment. Follow a consistent process for finding, screening, hiring, and onboarding new hires. One system I use for my business was Indeed. There are several more out there, but find the best system that works for you and fits your business needs.

Project Management System

The next system is a Project Management System. How the team will work the project, the responsibilities of each team player, and how the project will be managed. You can track progress of each job and team member. Basecamp, Teamwork, and Asana are just a few systems you can put in place for project management.

Analytics System

I coach a lot of people and most don't know what analytics are. Analytics is gathered information. Analytics is the discovery, interpretation, and communication of meaningful patterns of data.

With analytics, I am able to see who is viewing my pages, how my marketing is doing, and how people are responding to it. I use other platforms as well to test to see what works best for me.

Financial System

The final and one of the most important systems is a financial system. How people will get paid, manage contracts for clients, and anything dealing with the finances of your company. There are so many different financial management systems you can put in place. Quickbooks and Harvest are two really popular systems. A business owner should know how much money is left at the end of the month, what contributes to business success, and what the profit margins look like. This is when you really understand how numbers benefit and work for your business.

Sales tracking is keeping tabs on your sales activities. Sales tracking logs activities and provides you with information to create company success. Sales tracking means keeping good records and detailing all aspects of your sales process. Tracking your sales can let you know if you can scale up in business. You can't know what to do different unless you take stock of where the business stands.

Shift Point: "You have to have a tracking system in place to be a successful business owner."
Joyspeaks2u

To scale up in business is to grow or expand in a proportional growth of production and profit or large market position. Take a look at your business and see if you are ready for growth. Scalability is about capacity and capability. Scaling a business means setting the stage to enable and support growth in your company.

When I made a decision to scale up in my salon, I knew it was going to cost me money. I had an extra suite that needed to be rented out, but I knew if I allowed someone to rent that space out, I was going to have to make room for the increased clients that came with adding that new person. I had to do renovations to the salon, pay for new marketing, and position my business for the increase that would come with new upgrades and marketing. Scaling came with new planning, new systems, and technology.

I remember the time I did not properly prepare for scaling up in business. I was a new business and did not count the cost of having a full salon of workers. I opened the salon and within three months, I had a full staff. The hot water heater no longer got hot, the dryers kept cutting off, and the lobby was filled to capacity and I had to get more chairs.

I learned a lot from this decision to pack the salon, but not count the cost of what having a packed house would do. I did not have a proper system in place at the front desk for my girls that were on commission or technology that I needed for the revenue increase, customer increase and water.

I was not a favorable business owner at this time, but I was able to get the electrical problem to create more power in the dryer room within a week and get new system in place for the front desk that same week. It took a little longer to get a second hot water heater installed and parts we needed for the existing hot water heater. The part we needed was not in a store where my salon was located and a snow storm came the following week. It took almost a month to get the hot water heater resolved which met clients complaining, workers complaining, and more. It did not matter what was going on behind the scenes and that I was doing everything I could to resolve the hot water heater conflict quick, I lost money that week and had a group of angry staff.

It did not matter how much I apologized, I was going down in the books as the worst business owner ever that month. If I had to properly scale up, this would not have happen. This one of my best business lessons ever.

Systems are the ultimate method to turning a struggling business into thriving business. You can systemize virtual anything in your business. Every system you put in place can reduce stress, free up time, and enhance progress.

SHIFT ACTIVITY

What current systems do you have in place or you are going to put in place?

Chapter 17

Upgrade Your Branding

Shift Point: "A brand is a set of expectations, memories, stories, and relationships that, taken together, account for consumer's decision to choose one product or service over another." Seth Godin

When transitioning your business from self-employed to business ownership, we should see an upgraded shift in your marketing. A headshot from five years earlier needs to be updated. Website design might need to be upgraded or redone.

When business is going well, we sometimes neglect polishing up our marketing. It's just easy to be comfortable and make no changes to our branding.

I know sometimes in the beauty industry, stylist change looks weekly so different looks on flyers in the same year could work in this industry, but for other businesses and platforms, marketing a signature look for a season always works well. The signature look might be on your website, pop-up banner, or other marketing for a season and rebrand a different look for the next season if you choose to.

I usually brand a signature look for 12 months. Even if I do new pictures, I send my signature look to everyone that requires a head shot. My signature look is a short platinum cut like I am wearing on the back picture of this book cover. Figure out how to appeal to and attract the customers you want. I know I wanted to attract high end clients, Fortune 500, and major speaking platforms so I know a nice, short, and sassy cut with a platinum twist was going help me do that, still reflect my personality, and stand out above the rest. Your brand image should speak to the type of clients you want to attract.

Please be sure to get a professional photographer and invest in yourself to rebrand your business or add upgrades. If you're not a professional makeup artist or hair stylist, I recommend you get one for your professional headshots. If you are going to wear a wig, get it customized to fit your face.

Not only is it a good idea to brand a look in image, but in overall branding. When people know what to expect, they come to like and trust you. Once people trust your brand, they tell others about it and that yields an increase in sales and customers. This is considered as brand continuity and it's very important when shifting from self-employed to business ownership.

Branding is so much more than a logo or business card. That's just a part of it. Your brand represents all that you stand for as a company. It tells the story of why, how, and what you do. It communicates your personality and values. It helps your audience or community find you.

Your brand represents you if you are in front of someone or if you are not. How your company is viewed by the public is very important. Creating a strong brand will help you connect with your audience, create a community that believes in your vision, support your vision, and displays your style and creativity.

SHIFT POINT: "Great people build great brands."
Joyspeaks2u

SHIFT ASSIGNMENT: What upgrades have you made to your brand or plan to make to your brand? Create a timeline and budget to get it done.

_____

_____

_____

_____

_____

_____

_____

_____

_____

_____

_____

_____

Chapter 18

My Business No Longer Owns Me

I Own It

Shift Point: *"The two most popular warriors are patience and time."* **Leo Tolstoy**

My goal was to eventually get my salon to a place that would make it attractive to sell. In selling, you have to ask how you can build the business to make it more valuable for someone else. It's not how much money you make while you had the business, but the investor wants to know how much they will make after they purchase the business. One beautiful thing I had working for my salon business is most of my contractors had about a year left or close to a year so I had to sell while they were all in place. Once I restructure the business, I did not need a front desk person anymore, but still had my media team, marketing team, and personal assistant in place because I was already working on my new brand for my new business, I was starting once I sold the company. I had to make sure the business I wanted to sell still looked attractive in every way.

Prior to getting pregnant with my daughter, my salon was in a sweet place. I was making 2-3x what I needed to make to manage my business. It was in a great place of profit. I finally positioned myself to take a vacation and still got paid even if I was not there. I was no longer self-employed and trading time for money. I was now a business owner.

Being in business can be tough and some days are better than others but the time freedom is worth every sacrifice, being able to have my daughter go to the best schools, and being able to travel more has been a dream come true for me and my family. Everything you read so far was what I did to position me to transition from self -employed to business ownership.

It takes time to sell a business because you have to look at everything from paperwork, to financials, to adding more documentation to sell. I had amazing systems in place that ran without me and I was making money in my sleep. $1,000 days became my new norm.

I was in the business less and making more money. My V Collection wig and hair line was doing great. What I made off of one wig client was equivalent to what I would make doing 10 or more heads. I was truly working smarter and not harder.

Just within the salon business, I created seven income streams. The following income sources helped me retire from behind the chair and shift to business ownership: my money from hair clients, hair bundles from my line, girls that rented suites from me, wig income, t-shirts, hair retail product, and beauty industry classes. This did not include the other income that was not directly connected to my salon business. I made my first six figures in 2017. I have stocks, investments, or other things that also helped me maximize my revenue.

Another thing I did was position my business to receive contract work through my state. Based on the type of business you offer, you can also accept insurance. Since wigs were one of the services I offered, I positioned my business to become a vendor through local hospitals and insurance that paid for wigs for clients. It was indeed a process to get this done, but well worth the push towards business ownership.

Shift Point: "There will be unexpected things that happen in business that you did not think of." Joyspeaks2u

Things break, people leave, and unexpected financial things come up. That was happening when I was trying to sell. The air broke in the salon, the bathroom sink broke, and I had unexpected financial things going on at home. I had multiple streams of income working for me so it helped me to not be so stressed every time an unexpected financial situation occurred.

I kept great financials and had an amazing advisory team which consisted of my tax advisor, accountant and other mentors in my life. I added a lawyer and business broker to my team because I know for where I was going in life and in business, I was going to need both.

Once I did the numbers, projections, and looked at everything for selling the business, I took it to my advisory team who all were wealthy and most worked with numbers daily to get feedback, see if what I was asking in selling price was good, and just to identify any gaps. I could have missed. We added and took some things away and now it was time to work with attorney on drawing up other paperwork needed.

If you are considering selling, you will need some of the following documentation: Bill of Sales, cash flow statements, and offer to purchase agreement/assignment, profit and loss, balance sheet, lease, insurance policies, confidentiality agreement, and any other requested details about the business. Also, tax documents because people want to identify that what you are telling them is true because of numbers you are presenting for proof of additional documentation. Buyers may request other documentation like suppliers list, and contracts. Have every document to your business all filed together and organize everything to make the process of selling less hectic.

Let me just tell you, it was not a cake walk to sell my business. I learned so much during this process. I had never sold a business before so I sought help from experts in their individual fields to make the process smooth as could be.

Now I got the paperwork in place, I reached out to a few people I talked to over the last year that I thought would be interested and did face to face meetings. I sent them a confidentiality form before meeting in person so nothing discussed would get out because I did not make a big announcement I was selling and didn't let the people in my business know I was selling yet right away. It may not be that easy for you to identify buyers so you can hire a business broker or someone to help you find buyers to purchase.

I ended up seeking out help from a business broker after none of the people I met with went through with the deal. A Business Broker assists buyers and sellers privately held in business in buying and selling. They can also assist with estimate values for selling.

I had a closing date scheduled with one of my potential buyers and on the day of closing, she ignored my calls. I was pissed because of the amount of time I spent with her and she knew every number from my business.

Shift Point: "It's best to be silent until the deal is sealed in certain situations." Joyspeaks2u

Putting the news out that I was selling could have complicated things among the contactors that were renting from me.

Shift Assignment: List the people on your advisory team or people you want on your advisory team.

_____

_____

_____

_____

_____

_____

_____

_____

_____

_____

_____

_____

_____

_____

_____

_____

_____

_____

_____

_____

_____

_____

Chapter 19

Selling the Business

Shift Point: "Do what you have to do today so you can do what you want to do tomorrow." Joyspeaks2u

After four long months of people saying, "No," tears, and no real movement in the direction of selling the business, I felt like giving up. I had to make a decision if I was going to go into another lease because the month to month was much higher without having a lease. After praying, receiving encouragement from my husband and my advisory team, I started sharing my business with friends in my circle that had money and were always looking for investment opportunities.

The business broker I had in place didn't sell businesses that were asking for the price I wanted to sell for so instead of getting another business broker, I took the approach of talking to investors and people in my circle with money. I made them all complete confidentiality forms.

I spoke with my friend Jimmy one night on what I was trying to do and he said he would mention it to a few mutual associates we both knew to see if they would be interested. It never made it to that mutual friend. My friend Jimmy decided he wanted to look at It further. He brought some other team members that would do it with him on board and things started flowing in the direction of buying. I had to make a decision if I was going to renew my lease, go into a month to month, or submit a 30-day notice.

I decided on a month to month lease instead of going into another full year. The monthly increase amount made me work harder to get this business sold. If I went into another lease, everything was going to be different. I know there was going to be price increases and other changes. Another set of challenges came as I got closer to selling. I was holding strong to my faith because I know it would lead me to the things I hope for. *"Faith is the substance of things hoped for and the evidence of things not seen." (Hebrews 11:1)*

The property manager did not answer the phone, my e-mail responses were slow trying to get answers, and some of my girls contracts ended within 12 months. This made it harder to sell, but we finally started getting returned phone calls and e-mail responses. After finally getting responses to move this deal forward, one of the buyers got ill and she was the voice for the group and did all the communication. I continued to trust God that this salon was going to sell before 2017. We finally got calls and e-mail answer and schedule a closing date.

The first closing date got rescheduled and we made another date. We scheduled a 2nd closing date and I made arrangements to go to the beach this time because I just knew we were going to close. We met and everyone had their closing check with my name on it, but they still did not secure final documentation with property. I had no idea that this document was not secured, signed, and confirmed. No closing again. I walked out of Starbucks with my head held high in my cute closing outfit and the tears started to roll once I got in the parking lot.

We went to the beach to celebrate anyway and two days after being at the beach, I got the call that buyers were ready to finalize everything and wanted to keep our original Tuesday meeting that was supposed to happen after the last closing date. This meeting was designed to tell my old team that new managers were in charge. It actually happened. I sold my business. I was no longer the owner of Verve Hair and Body Spa.

Selling a business may not be for you, but just positioning your business for next level is what this book is all about. For me, selling that business was for my good and I knew my purpose required greater work from me. If you don't want to sell your business, make sure you know what the ultimate goal is so you can make the shift.

Chapter 20

THE SHIFT

Shift Point: *"Once you make it to a point of making it, you'll appreciate the struggle." Nas*

The reason you want to learn how to drive a stick shift is because it unlocks an entirely new world of driving. Many high performance cars are stick shift cars. With a stick shift, you will be rewarded with better fuel economy, greater reliability, improved performance and enhance control over the vehicle. A stick shift car is business ownership.

To shift is to move, change position, or direction. Another definition I like is to transfer from one place to another. When a shift takes place in your life whether in business or personal, everything around you shifted as well. When my business shifted, so did my friends, finances, and influence. Your mind is renewed and you operate and do things differently.

If you are looking to grow your business, increase your customer base and make more money, business ownership is the way to go. My ultimate goal was time and financial freedom. Don't think once you are out of the business, you are out of the business. Once you have transitioned to business ownership, finances should increase which means the amount you pay in taxes will increase along with paperwork. At this point, you should have an advisory team to include: attorney, accountant, and prayer partners.

Making the shift in business takes time and effort. It is not an overnight process and you will not do everything right and unexpected things will happen.

After selling the business, there were still things I had to deal with because even after hiring help for the documentation, there was still a major error that I did not catch, my attorney, or buyer's attorney. It was caught after the deal was closed. I had an attorney on my advisory team so I went to him to assist me with this matter at hand and it made the process much better.

I am now the owner of my new baby Touch of Joy International, LLC where I travel the world and speak and coach on Entrepreneurship, Leadership, and Financial Literacy. I do empowerment speaking and help companies with organizational leadership and development. That's right guys, I jumped back in the water, re-build a company from the ground up with a toddler and a husband. That's another book.

The beautiful thing about starting this time is I am building business credit, I started with more capital, and now I am working towards purchasing a building and not renting it. People still get confused as to how I sold a business when I was renting a building, but I sold the brand, the business concept, and the revenue potential. I turned the business into an asset because of the systems I put in place. Building a business starts without a building. It has to make sense before the doors open.

Final Thoughts

In business, we have to know when to shift gears, take a step back, and when to accelerate. Stop signs and distractions will present themselves while you're traveling from self-employed to business ownership. With insurance, great paperwork, and a team, problems can be minimized when they come. Always hire your weakness, have mentors, and experts on your team for different subject matters. You can't do big vision along!

SHIFT POINT: "You never know what results will come from your action. But if you do nothing, there will be no results." Mahatma Gandhi

Making the Shift Master Mind Program

Making the Shift Mastermind Program is a six- month program designed to help you make the shift from self-employed to business ownership. This program starts in February 2019 and there are only 10 spots available.

Having this book and using the code word SHIFT gets you a discount off the Making the Shift Mastermind Program cost. Call 1-800-570-3544 or email info@touchofjoy.org to see if you qualify.

About the Author

JOYSPEAKS2u

Joy McLaughlin-Harris is a native of Gadsden, South Carolina. Mrs. Harris is the founder of Touch of Joy, International, Touch of Joy Youth Foundation, and Hannah Joy Collection. Mrs. Harris has an Associates of Arts Degree, Bachelor of Psychology, and Master in Organizational Leadership and Development. Outside of being a successful entrepreneur, she is a renowned Published Author, Certified Financial Literacy Coach, Community Activist, Wife and Mother.

In 2011, Joy was nominated and crowned as one of Columbia, South Carolina's Phenomenal Women. In 2016, she was recognized by the Beauty Association and featured in Pastor's Journal Magazine for her generous work in the community. Joy continues to work hard each day creating a platform for women of color to express their voice as community leaders and successful entrepreneurs.

Joy approaches everyday by the motto, "Failure is part of the process, only if you believe the process is part of your destiny."

For Booking:
Call 1-800-570-3544
Touchofjoy.org
info@touchofjoy.org